Wakeboarding

by Stephen Timblin

Published by The Child's World®
1980 Lookout Drive
Mankato, MN 56003-1705
800-599-READ
www.childsworld.com

The Child's World®: Mary Berendes, Publishing Director
Shoreline Publishing Group, LLC: James Buckley Jr.,
    Production Director
The Design Lab: Design and production

ISBN: 978-1-60973-186-1
LCCN: 2011928876

Photo credits: Cover: Photos.com.
Interior: AP/Wide World: 24, 28; Corbis: 4, 8, 11, 12,
23; dreamstime.com/Anthonyata: 15; Getty Images/
Quinn Rooney: 27; Photos.com: 7, 16, 19, 20.

Printed in the United States of America
Mankato, Minnesota
July, 2011
PA02094

Table of Contents

Danny Harf shows the skill and daring needed in wakeboarding.

CHAPTER ONE

Up in the Air!

On September 9, 2008, Danny Harf had a single goal in mind—become the first wakeboarder ever to land a 1260. That's a trick requiring an incredible *three and a half* spins in the air.

More than a dozen times the day before, Danny had charged the wake left by his speedboat. (A wake is the set of waves left behind a boat as it cuts through the water.) He launched like rocket into the air, only to crash land. Today, he'd already jammed his finger on one spill and whacked his face on another.

With the boat ahead of him at top speed, Danny popped off the wake one more time. Passing the towrope behind his back, he spun once. Twice. Three times. With a final half-spin Danny landed on the tail of his board! He stood up and pointed to the sky while riding on. Danny had done it! Within hours, word had spread across the Internet and riders across the world about Danny's amazing feat.

How did wakeboarding get so hot? The sport didn't start overnight—not even close. Indeed, the sport **evolved** so slowly that picking the moment that wakeboarding began is impossible.

Wakeboarding is a thrilling, high-speed water sport.

Surfers started the sport by getting tow rides from fast boats.

Most riders agree that surfers helped start wakeboarding. Surfers spend much of their time waiting for big waves to appear in the ocean. And as early as the 1920s, surfers would play around waiting for these waves by having boats tow them on their boards. This was never considered a real sport. It was just a fun way to pass the time.

In the 1980s, surfers in Australia and New Zealand began building smaller boards. They were designed to be towed by boats. They called them "skurf boards." The riders held onto towropes like water skiers. These riders were just towed around, but the real fun was in skimming over and across the boat's wake. The wake was like a never-ending wave for the surf-hungry riders.

In 1985, a surfboard shop owner named Tony Finn started building and selling these boards. His "Skurfers" quickly became popular, and within a few years friendly competitions were being held.

The Skurfer, though, was hard to handle. Soon, people created new board designs that were easier to ride. The most important early inventions were straps that kept a riders feet in place on the board. Interestingly, two designers can take credit for this key invention. Tony Finn and another rider named Jimmy Redmon added straps to their board designs at the same time—while working and riding thousands of miles apart! In 1989, Redmon created the World Wakeboard Association (WWA), an organization that organizes and supports wakeboarding around the globe.

Tony Finn shows off the Skurfer, his invention that helped wakeboarding grow quickly.

Adding wakeboarding to the
X Games helped make it part of
a growing action-sports world.

The 1990s was a huge decade for wakeboarding. Both skateboarding and snowboarding had become popular activities. Wakeboarders started bringing tricks from those two board sports onto the water. Professional riders like Darin Shapiro, Scott Byerly, and Shaun Murray (see Chapter 3) turned the spotlight onto wakeboarding. They were able to launch themselves out of the water with stylish spins, **board grabs**, and sky-high flips. In 1996, wakeboarding was included in the ESPN X Games for the first time alongside skateboarding and BMX biking.

In the 2000s, wakeboarding's popularity peaked as riders began regularly landing tricks with wild names like 1080s and Half Cab Double Back Rolls. Tricks like those and Danny's were once considered impossible. Where top riders will take wakeboarding from here is anyone's guess, though one thing's for certain— wakeboarding's future is up in the air!

CHAPTER TWO

Wakeboarding Gear Guide

Wakeboarding isn't the kind of sport you can just jump into, unless you have a board and a boat and a lake in your backyard. Wakeboarding actually needs a great deal of gear.

The first thing you need, of course, is a wakeboard. The first wakeboards were modeled after surfboards. Designs have changed greatly over the last two decades, however. Modern boards are more like a **hybrid** of snowboards, surfboards, and water-skis. These wakeboards come in several different lengths and shapes. The rounder a board is, the smoother it will ride and turn in the water. Boards with sharper edges and a more square-shaped nose and tail are harder to ride, but pop off the wake with more force.

Here's a good look at the wakeboard, boots, and tow rope . . . in midair!

Look for the small fins on the bottom of the wakeboard.

The inside of a wakeboard is light plastic or foam to make the board **buoyant** (BOY-yant), meaning it will float instead of sink in water. This core is surrounded by fiberglass. This strong but light stuff keeps the weight of the board down but adds strength. This strength is **vital**. Wakeboards take quite a beating skipping over and landing on water at high speeds.

Like a surfboard, a wakeboard has fins on the bottom. These fins play a big part in how the board rides through the water. Older boards used to have just a single large fin at the back of the board. Today, wakeboards have several smaller fins. These help riders keep more stable and turn more smoothly in the water. On many boards, riders can switch their fin set-up to match their riding style. Shorter fins let a rider spin on the water more easily, while longer fins keep the board more stable.

Like a snowboard, there are **bindings** on the topside of a wakeboard. The original wakeboard bindings were simple straps for rider's feet to slide under. Nowadays, bindings are as advanced as the boards themselves. Most look like boots attached to the top of the board. They feature laces or Velcro straps to keep riders' feet snugly in place.

Along with a wakeboard, riders need a few other key pieces of equipment before getting out onto the water. The first is a towrope, which is attached to the back of the boat pulling the rider. The line on a towrope is typically around 70-feet (21-m) long, and ends with a rubber or plastic handle that the rider holds onto. All riders should wear a life-vest with a good fit. Many riders wear helmets also.

This series of shots shows how a wakeboarder uses the wake as a kind of ramp for jumping.

Boats or Jet Skis give the wakeboarder speed and power.

That leaves one last piece of equipment—the boat. A wakeboarder without a boat is like a kite without wind. While most powerboats can be used to pull a wakeboarder, specially designed wakeboarding boats are the best. Such boats have a wakeboard tower, which is a steel or aluminum frame that the towrope is attached to. Raising the rope up or down the tower lets riders get up on the board more easily. It also can give them more control and height on jumps. Wakeboarding boats also come with a system that lets the driver lower the boat deeper into the water. This creates a bigger wake for launching riders.

CHAPTER THREE

Legends of the Wake

Will there ever be a wakeboarder as famous as skateboarder Tony Hawk? Probably not. But that doesn't matter to most wakeboarders. What's important to them is earning the respect of fellow riders while taking the sport to new heights. For these riders, breaking new ground with a fresh trick will always outshine any trophies or victory parades.

Here are some of the top riders in the history of the wakeboarding.

- Amber Wing. This hard-riding Australian is the first woman wakeboarder to land both a **toeside** 720 and a 900! In 2010, *Transworld Wakeboarding* magazine honored Amber with their Female Rider of the Year award.

Amber Wing shows off her award-winning style.

Dallas Friday's stardom helped spread the word about wakeboarding.

- Dallas Friday. A gymnast turned rider, Dallas began competing professionally when she was 13 years old. From 2001 through 2009, Dallas was voted the #1 female rider in the *Wakeboarding* Magazine Readers Poll. And in 2004, she won the ESPN ESPY Award for Best Female Action Sports Athlete of the Year.

- Darin Shapiro. One of wakeboarding's first great riders, Darin began riding in 1991. Darin is a four-time world wakeboarding champion and has three X Games gold medals. In his mid-30s, he now runs a popular wakeboarding camp.

- Harley Clifford. Only 17 years old, Harley is one of the youngest riders on the pro wakeboarding tour. That didn't stop him from winning numerous events in 2010 with insanely tough tricks like a Mobe 720. Harley ended the year on a high note by being named *Transworld Wakeboarding* magazine's Best Wakeboarder of the Year.

- Scott Byerly: Scott is one of the greatest trick creators in wakeboarding history. Moves invented by Scott include the Pete Rose (a toeside back roll with frontside 360) and the Fat Chance (a **heelside** front flip with a frontside 360).

Young Harley Clifford has a great future ahead of him in his favorite sport.

Veteran wakeboard star Shaun Murray invented some of today's top tricks.

- Shaun Murray. A four-time world champion rider, Shaun ruled the world of wakeboarding in the late 1990s and early 2000s. Shaun was the first rider to nail a 900 and was also the star rider in the wakeboarding video game *Wakeboarding Unleashed*.

The stars of wakeboarding are continuing to invent new tricks. They use their imagination—and a little gymnastic skill—to make their days on the lake ones for everyone to remember.

Glossary

bindings—name for the straps or boots that hold a rider's feet to a wakeboard or to skis

board grabs—tricks in which the rider reaches down to hold the board with his hand while flying through the air

buoyant—able to float on water

evolved—developed over time

heelside—describing tricks that begin on the side of the board closest to the rider's heels

hybrid—a blend or combination

toeside—describing tricks that begin on the side of the board closest to the rider's toes

vital—important

BOOKS

Danny Harf: Wakeboarding Superstar
By Christopher Goranson. New York, NY: Rosen Central, 2005.
Find out more about this trailblazing athlete.

Extreme Wakeboarding
By Bobbie Kalman. New York, NY: Crabtree, 2006.
Including descriptions of key tricks and top events, this book explores
the competitive world of wakeboarding.

WEB SITES

For links to learn more about extreme sports: **childsworld.com/links**

Note to Parents, Teachers, and Librarians: We routinely verify our Web
links to make sure they are safe and active sites. So encourage your
readers to check them out!

Index

About the Author

When it comes to board sports, **Stephen Timblin** would rather be snowboarding. He has written numerous books for readers of all ages, and enjoys spending time with his beautiful twin daughters.